Lands of our Ancestors Book Three

Teacher's Guide

Developed by Fred Messecar
and Gary Robinson

P.O. Box 1123 / Santa Ynez, CA 93460
www.tribaleyeproductions.com

© 2019 Tribal Eye Productions
ISBN 978-0-9800272-9-7
All Rights Reserved

TABLE OF CONTENTS

1. Introduction to the Teacher Guide	p. 5
2. Fourth Grade HSS Standards	p. 6
3. Overview of Gold Rush Period and Early California Statehood	p. 8
4. Accuracy of Events Portrayed	p. 10
5. Images Depicting the Era	p. 11
6. Geographical Locations in Book Three	p. 14
7. Information Sources on the Chumash Gold Rush and Early Statehood	p. 15
8. Characters & Relationships	p. 16
9. Timeline of Events	p. 17
10. Chapter Questions & Answers Words to Know for Each Chapter	p. 21
11. Student Projects	p. 45

4

Lands of Our Ancestors Book Three
Teacher's Guide Introduction

This Teacher's Guide is designed to enrich teaching <u>Lands of Our Ancestors Book Three</u> across the curriculum. After this introduction, the guide begins with the California Content Standards for 4th grade History-Social Sciences the book addresses. This will provide teachers with important information about what the focus should be in teaching the Mexican-American War, Gold Rush and Early Statehood periods.

Section Three contains Overviews of the periods addressed in Book Three. This is followed by a section that validates the accuracy of the events portrayed in <u>Book Three</u>. Section Five provides pages of Images of Life during the era. These images help illustrate the story for students. Because the characters relocate several times during the story, Section Six is a list of the main geographic locations of the book.

Next, the guide provides a list of additional sources of information about the Chumash people, the Gold Rush and Statehood, if needed, for further research.

The next section of the guide contains the same "Characters and Relationships" reference as well as the "Timeline" found in the book. Section ten, the largest section of this guide, contains "Questions, Answers, and Words to Know" for each chapter of <u>Book Three</u>. The questions can be used in teacher-directed class discussions, small group discussions, or as written work. The variety of questions in each chapter align with The Six Levels of Questioning: knowledge, comprehension, application, analysis, synthesis, evaluation. Answers are provided for all chapter questions. New vocabulary, including words from the Samala Chumash, other tribes, and Spanish languages, are found in each chapter's "Words to Know" section.

Near the end, to extend the learning after the book is completed, the guide includes possible project choices to engage students. The projects are designed to meet the needs of the diverse learners found in most classrooms. Each project meets a specific fourth grade History-Social Science Content Standard for California Public Schools.

Students who complete reading the story, discuss or write responses to the questions, and learn the new vocabulary words will meet a variety of the fourth grade California Common Core State Standards in reading, writing, and language.

California 4th Grade History Social-Science Standards

Students should be able to answer these questions:

- How did the discovery of gold change California?
- How did California become part of the United States?
- Why did people come to California?

4.3 Students explain the economic, social, and political life in California from the establishment of the Bear Flag Republic through the Mexican-American War, the Gold Rush, and the granting of statehood.

1. Identify the locations of Mexican settlements in California and those of other settlements, including Fort Ross and Sutter's Fort.

2. Compare how and why people traveled to California and the routes they traveled (e.g., James Beckwourth, John Bidwell, John C. Fremont, Pio Pico).

3. Analyze the effects of the Gold Rush on settlements, daily life, politics, and the physical environment (e.g., using biographies of John Sutter, Mariano Guadalupe Vallejo, Louise Clapp).

4. Study the lives of women who helped build early California (e.g., Biddy Mason).

5. Discuss how California became a state and how its new government differed from those during the Spanish and Mexican periods.

We recommend also consulting the **California History Social Studies Framework** for additional background information. The framework focuses on the Gold Rush and Statehood beginning on page 77 of the PDF version, which can be found online at: https://www.cde.ca.gov/ci/hs/cf/documents/hssfwchapter7.pdf

California Common Core Language Arts Standards

Vocabulary:

- CCSS.ELA-LITERACY.L.4.4

Determine or clarify the meaning of unknown and multiple-meaning words and phrases based on grade 4 reading and content, choosing flexibly from a range of strategies.

- CCSS.ELA-LITERACY.L.4.6

Acquire and use accurately grade-appropriate general academic and domain-specific words and phrases, including those that signal precise actions, emotions, or states of being (e.g., quizzed, whined, stammered) and that are basic to a particular topic (e.g., *wildlife, conservation,* and *endangered* when discussing animal preservation).

Comprehension:

- CCSS.ELA-LITERACY.RL.4.1

Refer to details and examples in a text when explaining what the text says explicitly and when drawing inferences from the text.

- CCSS.ELA-LITERACY.RL.4.2

Determine a theme of a story, drama, or poem from details in the text; summarize the text.

- CCSS.ELA-LITERACY.RL.4.3

Describe in depth a character, setting, or event in a story or drama, drawing on specific details in the text (e.g., a character's thoughts, words, or actions).

Overview of the Mexican-American War, Gold Rush and Early Statehood

In the 1840s, more immigrants from the United States and other countries began to arrive in Alta California, and Mexico was having trouble maintaining control of the territory. At the same time, Mexico was also having territorial troubles in another region, Texas, as the United States aggressively sought to expand its own lands. This led to war between the U.S and Mexico.

The Mexican–American War took place from 1846 to 1848, but most of the fighting happened outside California. This war followed in the wake of the 1845 annexation of Texas by the U.S., after the Texas Revolution a decade earlier.

About the same time, troubles between American settlers and Mexicans in Alta California had begun in earnest. In June of 1846 a band of Americans revolted, took over the city of Sonoma and jailed the Mexican governor, Mariano Guadalupe Vallejo. They raised the "Bear Flag" for the first time in the state. Then, acting on information that the English and Russians were planning to move in, American Commodore John Drake Sloat anchored in Monterey, the capital of Alta California, and raised the American flag. Sloat and his crew met no resistance from those living in Monterey. Approximately one-third of the northern half of Mexico, including California, became part of the United States after the U.S. defeated Mexico in 1848.

Just as the war was ending, James Marshall, an employee of immigrant landowner John Sutter, discovered a little nugget of gold at Sutter's lumber mill on the American River in Coloma, California. News of the discovery spread like wildfire worldwide, bringing some 300,000 gold-seekers to the territory. The sudden influx of money and people allowed American settlers to quickly move toward statehood.

The effects of the Gold Rush were substantial. Whole indigenous societies were attacked, decimated and pushed off their ancient lands by gold-seekers, called "forty-niners" in reference to the peak year of the Gold Rush immigration, 1849. San Francisco was the primary arrival point for those coming by sea, and the sleepy seaside village morphed into a major metropolis within a few short years. Those traveling by land often came over the Sierra Nevada Mountains by stagecoach, wagon train and later, locomotive.

The Gold Rush also caused irreparable environmental destruction through the introduction of hydraulic mining in the 1850s, which clogged and polluted rivers throughout the state, at great cost to the affected farmers and Native American villages downstream.

In the political arena, in 1849, delegates from around California gathered in Monterey, then the capital, to write a constitution for the new state. That constitution copied substantial portions of constitutions of other states as well as the U.S. Constitution, but also contained original provisions. The new constitution was ratified by popular vote later that same year, and Congress made California the thirty-first state in September, 1850.

As settlers continued to flood the state, Native Americans continued to suffer. Native inhabitants were often forcibly removed from their tribal lands by incoming miners, ranchers and farmers. Additionally, more than three hundred massacres of California Indians were carried out, while disease and starvation also took heavy tolls.

The new state government encouraged the process by passing laws that stripped Indians of rights while enabling non-Indians to buy and sell Indians as laborers. California's first Governor, Peter Burnet, openly called for a "war of extermination" of indigenous peoples while the state legislature provided the means of funding militias to carry out this policy. Between 1850 and 1860, the state paid out around one and a half million dollars for "expeditions against Indians."

Sources: An American Genocide; Wikipedia; California History-Social Science Framework

Accuracy of Events Portrayed in <u>Lands of our Ancestors Book Three</u>

This work of historical fiction depicts what might have happened to California Native Americans as Alta California transitioned from Mexican control in the 1840s to US/American control in 1850 and beyond. Although the characters and the specific plot are fictional, the people and events in the book are based on historical documents and the historical writings of non-fiction authors and scholars.

More specifically, for example, some of the details of the lives of California Indians during the Gold Rush era came directly from the non-fiction personal narrative <u>Unwritten History: Life Among the Modocs</u>, written by Joaquin Miller and first published in 1873. Facts regarding the campaigns to slaughter California Natives from the end of the Mexican-American War to the early years of California statehood came from early California newspapers and <u>An American Genocide: The United States and the California Indian Catastrophe</u>, written by Benjamin Madley, published in 2016.

However the period is depicted, the truth is that the Gold Rush and the early years of California statehood contributed heavily to the further destruction and devastation of Native American peoples, communities and cultures in the region that became known as California.

Images of California Life
Mid 1840s - 1855

Larkin House, Monterey. Built three blocks from the bay in 1835 by American merchant Thomas Larkin. It was the first two-story house in Monterey. Larkin operated a store from the back of the house. This is where Alapay reconnected with her Mexican friend, Magdalena.

This is a typical horse-drawn cargo wagon like the ones described on page 36. These vehicles were the delivery trucks of their day.

Sutter's famous lumber mill at Coloma, CA, on the American River where gold flakes were discovered in January, 1848. Geological forces working over millions of years produced high concentrations of the metal in this region of California, which was the ancient homeland of the Nisenan Indian people.

Images of California Life
Mid 1840s - 1855, continued

Pictured to the left is a method of gold-mining known as sluicing. Water from a riverbed is diverted into the sluice, allowing miners to pan for gold in the river's dry gravel bed. Groups of miners maintained camps near rivers and streams, tearing down and rebuilding the sluices as they cleared all the gold from a section of the river.

This image portrays the hydraulic method of gold mining as depicted on page 128 of <u>Lands of our Ancestors Book Three</u>. Many of the methods of mining gold destroyed the environment and made it impossible for plants, animals and fish to survive nearby.

San Francisco, 1850. After the discovery of gold in Alta California, San Francisco was transformed from a sleeping little seaside village into a major international city within two years. It was the main arrival point for gold seekers traveling by sea from all over the world.

Images of California Life
Mid 1840s - 1855, continued

Single shot, muzzle-loading pistol like the ones captured by Kilik and the people of Tukuyun's village described in chapter four.

Colt 44 caliber revolver like the one Henry used to free Alapay on page 145. The single shot musket style pistol was no match for this innovation in weaponry.

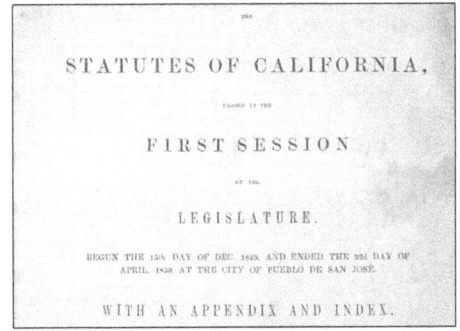

The newly created California state legislature wasted no time in passing laws that stripped Native Americans of their rights to land and liberty while giving other state citizens the ability to purchase Indians for labor.

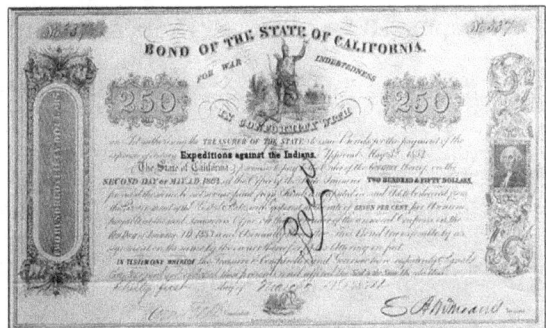

The new state government also provided the means to finance "Expeditions against the Indians" such as issuing bonds for sale to the public. This example bond had a value of $250. Around 1 million dollars was paid to militias that murdered thousands of California Indians.

These are the ruins of La Purisima Mission, which, like most of the Spanish missions, had been abandoned by the 1850s. As described on pages 171-174, Kilik's family passed by several mission ruins on their return journey to their homeland. A few California Indians somehow managed to miraculously survive the successive invasions of outsiders intent on taking the lands and resources of the area's original inhabitants.

Geographic Locations in Book Three

Chapter 1 Cuyama Valley, Southern San Joaquin Valley

Chapter 2 Kern River, Western foothills of the Sierra Nevada Mountains

Chapter 3 King River

Chapter 4 Western Sierra Nevada Mountains

Chapter 5 Monterey

Chapter 6 Monterey and surrounding ranchos

Chapter 8 Monterey and surrounding ranchos

Chapter 9 Monterey and surrounding ranchos

Chapter 10 San Joaquin Delta and its tributary river system

Chapter 11 San Francisco, American River

Chapter 12 South Fork of the American River; South of Folsom, CA

Chapter 13 Kosumme (Cosumnes) and Mokelumne Rivers

Chapter 14 Western Sierra Nevada Mountains

Chapter 15 Stockton, French Camp, Fresno

Chapter 16 Lake Tulare (now a dry lake bed), Mission San Luis Obispo, Mission La Purisima Concepcíon, Mission Santa Inez, and the Santa Ynez Valley

Sources on the Chumash People:

1. California's Chumash Indians, A Project of the Santa Barbara Museum of Natural History; EZ Nature Books; 1992, Revised Edition 2002.

2. The Chumash, Seafarers of the Pacific Coast; Karen Bush Gibson; Capstone Press, 2004.

3. "The Samala People" (DVD); produced by the Santa Ynez Band of Chumash Indians; Available from the tribe's Culture Department; 805-688-7997.

4. Bad Indians: A Tribal Memoir; Deborah A. Miranda; Heyday, 2013.

5. Samala-English Dictionary-A Guide to the Samala Language of the Ineseno Chumash People; Santa Ynez Band of Chumash Indians with Richard Applegate, PhD; 2007.

6. Website: www.sbnature.org/research/anthro/chumash/intro.htm (Chumash section of the Santa Barbara Museum of Natural History's website)

7. Website: www.santaynezchumash.org/history.html (The Santa Ynez Band of Chumash Indians official website)

8. Wikipedia Website: https://en.wikipedia.org/wiki/Chumash_people.

Sources on the Gold Rush and Statehood in California:

1. Unwritten History: Life Among the Modocs; Joaquin Miller; Orion Press, 1972; first printed 1873.

2. An American Genocide: The United States and the California Indian Catastrophe; Benjamin Madley; Yale University Press, 2016.

3. The Conflict Between the California Indian and the White Population; Sherburne F. Cook; University of California Press, 1976.

4. The Destruction of California Indians; Robert F. Heizer; University of Nebraska Press, 1974; republished by Bison Books, 1993.

Characters and Relationships in the <u>Lands of our Ancestors</u> series

Kilik (Miguel) – main character, son of Solomol and Wonono

Tuhuy (Rafael) – Kilik's cousin, son of Salapay and Yol

Stuk (Maria) – Kilik's younger sister

Solomol (Salvador) - Kilik's father

Salapay – Tuhuy's father

Wonono – Kilik's mother

Yol (Yolanda) – Tuhuy's mother

Tah-chi – Yokuts Indian scout for the Place of Condors village

Kai-ina – (Yokuts) Kilik's second wife, mother of Malik

Taya – Tuhuy's wife

Alapay (Andrea) – Tuhuy's daughter and Malik's cousin

Malik (Mateo) – Kilik's son and Andrea's cousin

Diego – Native outlaw and leader of Indians who attacked ranches

Magdalena Pacheco – Ranch owner's daughter who befriends Alapay

Limik – (Yokuts – Hawk) Kai-ina's father

Tukuyun – (Yokuts - Jackrabbit) Chief of one of the Yokuts bands

Loknee – (Miwok – Rain Falling Through) Chief of one of the Miwok bands

Mariposa – (Butterfly – Spanish) Miwok woman who marries Malik

Henry Jamieson – American newspaper reporter

Timeline of Historical and Fictional Events in the Lands of our Ancestors series

1769	First mission established in San Diego
1776	Solomol is born at the "Place of River Turtles" village
1777	Salapay is born at " " " " "
1780	Solomol's wife Wonono is born at the "Place of River Turtles" village
1781	Salapay's wife Yol is born at the "Place of River Turtles" village
1792	Kilik is born at " " " "
1793	Tuhuy is born at " " " "
1797	Kilik's sister Stuk is born at " " "
1804	Kilik & family go to mission
1804-05	Kilik & family experience hardships in the mission
1806	Children escape the mission on Summer Solstice morning (June)

Book 1 Ends

1806	Arrive at "Place of Condors" village
1811	Kilik marries Lau-lau (Yokuts) – Kilik is 19
1812	Earthquake damages missions in Chumash territory
	Baby is born to Kilik night of earthquake, but mom & baby die
1813	Stuk dies from measles brought to village by visitor
1814	Tuhuy leaves village to live alone, study healing, hermit
	Kilik leaves village to explore the region
1819	Kilik returns to village –
	Tuhuy returns to village, sees Taya (several years younger)
1820	Tuhuy marries Taya (Coastal Chumash) Tuhuy is 27
	Simultaneous ceremony: Kilik marries Kai-ina (Yokuts)
1821	Malik is born to Kilik who is 29 years old & Kai-ina
	Mexico wins independence
1822	'Alapay is born to Tuhuy and Taya

1823	Cousins Malik and "Alapay play together
1824	Kilik begins raiding ranches and missions for cattle – age 32
1825-30	'Alapay blends healing and fighting as needed
1832	Kilik turns 40
1833	Tuhuy turns 40
1833	Kilik begins to train 12-year-old Malik as hunter & warrior
	'Alapay wants to learn too
	Spanish padres expelled from missions – Mission Indians released
	Pacheco gets major land grant – needs laborers
	Epidemic outbreak (flu)
1834-1848	Mexican Rancho Period
1834	Pacheco's men raid Condor Village; take Tuhuy and others to Ranch
	Tuhuy and everyone held at ranch, must work
	Kilik finds crippled father, brings him and aunt Yol back
	Kilik raids ranches, looks for family, considered outlaw by Ranchers
	Kilik and Deigo raid Rancho Caballero, rescue the Family
	Hidden Place is attacked twice by Mexican forces, but defeated
	The Family leaves Hidden Place village and heads northward

Book 2 Ends

1835-1840	The Family travels northward to escape further troubles
1840	Settle near Monterey, capital of California under Spain & Mexico
	Posing as a Mexican, Malik (Mateo) gets job as Vaquero
	Family realizes they must have Mexican last names
1842	Alapay (Andrea) miraculously reconnects with Magdalena who helps
	Alapay gets a job in Monterey and learns some English
1846	U.S. ship sails into Monterey Bay/ Malik and Alapay return to their village
1846-48	Mexican-American War; Mexico conquered

1848	War ends – Treaty signed / New Gov't set up in Monterey
	Gold discovered on Sutter's land
	Malik is 27 – 'Alapay is 26
	American miners begin displacing & attacking Indians
1849	Gold Rush / International mix of miners invade Northern CA
	San Francisco transforms from little village to international city
1850	State Constitution Convention
	CA becomes a state
	First state governor (Peter Burnett) declares a war of extermination on Indians, and bonds were issued to raise funds to pay for this extermination
	Act for the Governance & Protection of Indians passed (this act allowed for sale and indentured servitude of CA Indians)
1851-52	CA tribes sign 18 treaties with US that were never ratified
1853	Federal Gov't begins establishing military reservations where Indians could live in isolation and protection from the general population
1854	State capital moves to Sacramento
1855	Church gives back small portion of land to Samala Chumash
	Several Native families settle on this land
	Kilik is 63 years old/Solomol is 79
1856	Kilik's family returns to the Place of River Turtles
	Solomol dies and is buried at the Place of River Turtles
	Baby born to Mariposa
	Baby born to Alapay

Chapter Questions & Answers

Words to Know for Each Chapter

Chapter 1 - Wearing Disguises (Page 7-16)

Words to Know:

1. disguises- to modify the manner or appearance of (a person, for example) in order to prevent from being recognized.
2. Alta California (Spanish)- high or upper California
3. notorious- known widely and usually unfavorably.
4. destination- the place to which one is going or directed.
5. sour- having the characteristics of smelling of decay.
6. resentment- indignation or ill will stemming from a feeling of having been wronged or offended.
7. foreign- located away from one's native country.
8. mass- a large but nonspecific amount or number.
9. trenches- a long narrow ditch embanked with its own soil and used for concealment and protection in warfare.
10. yield- to give up (an advantage, for example) to another.
11. motley- having elements of great variety or incongruity.
12. intrusion- an inappropriate or unwelcome addition.
13. livestock- domestic animals, such as cattle or horses, raised for home use or for profit, especially on a farm.
14. meager- deficient in quantity, fullness, or extent; scanty.
15. conceal- to keep from being observed or discovered; hide.
16. passage- movement from one place to another.
17. talisman- an object marked with spiritual importance and believed to confer on its bearer supernatural powers or protection.
18. reverently- marked by, feeling, or expressing reverence.
19. outcropping- a portion of bedrock or other stratum protruding through the soil level.
20. caravan- a company of travelers journeying together, as across a desert or through hostile territory.
21. *Hola* (Spanish)- hello
22. *Señor* (Spanish)- sir

*Questions with Answers:

1. Why did Kilik, Tuhuy and their families leave the village known as the Hidden Place?
   - Mexican government/Mexican military knew where the village was located and they knew they would be attacked again.
2. What is the reason Kilik and Tuhuy's families go in a different direction than Diego and his group?
   - They decided to go north where Kai-ina's people were from and had heard it was safer.
3. What is the talisman that Kilik gives to Malik? Where did it come from, and why is it important to Malik?
   - Piece of antler with deer hide string (necklace).
   - Blessed by a ceremonial leader at the Place of River Turtles.
   - Given to Malik by his father Kilik who wore it all his life.
4. What disguises did the group wear to trick the caravan of Mexican merchants? Where did those disguises come from?
   - Clothing from the Mexicans.
   - Clothing was taken from the dead bodies who had attacked the Hidden Place.
5. What was missing and needed to complete the groups' disguises in case they came across more caravans?
   - Leather shoes.

*Student answers will vary but should mention these key details in their responses. This is true for answers to all chapter questions throughout this guide.

Chapter 2 - A Home Among the Yokuts (Page 17-28)

Words to Know:

1. incident- a particular occurrence, especially one of minor importance.
2. devastated- to overwhelm; confound; stun.
3. introductions- the act or process of introducing or the state of being introduced.
4. astonishment- great surprise or amazement.
5. precede- to be in front of or prior to in order.
6. exploits- an act or deed, especially a brilliant or heroic one.
7. fascination- the capability of eliciting intense interest or of being very attractive.
8. momentarily- for a moment or an instant.
9. embrace- to clasp or hold close with the arms, usually as an expression of affection.
10. drought- a long period of abnormally low rainfall, especially one that adversely affects growing or living conditions.
11. consulting- to seek advice or information of.
12. relocate- to move to or establish in a new place.
13. concentration- the act or process of concentrating, especially the fixing of close, undivided attention.
14. inevitable- impossible to avoid or prevent; certain to happen.
15. destination- the place to which one is going or directed.
16. suspicious- arousing or apt to arouse suspicion; questionable.
17. impatient- unable to wait patiently or tolerate delay; restless.
18. faltered- to be unsteady in purpose or action, as from loss of courage or confidence; waver.
19. seize- To take by force; capture or conquer.
20. *Indios* (Spanish)- Indians, Native Americans
21. reins- two long narrow straps attached to each end of the bit of a bridle and used by a rider or driver to control a horse or other animal.

Questions:

1. What strange and wonderful connection did Kilik and Limik, Kai-ina's father, have?
    - Both of their names translate to hawk or falcon.

2. What natural features make the village, Place Above, such a safe place?
   - Long winding path that leads to a flat place that overlooks the valley below.
3. Why did the Native people from Place Above need to leave after years of relatively peaceful living?
   - Signs in the night sky warned of danger.
   - Sources of food and water were drying up.
4. As the group traveled northward, what signal meant danger? What signal meant it was safe?
   - Coyote wail meant danger.
   - Magpie warble meant all clear.
   - Hawk screech warned 1 or 2 people were coming.
5. Why, when meeting a caravan while traveling, did the groups' disguises not work this time?
   - The Mexican soldiers knew they were disguised Indians because they had no last names.

Chapter 3 - The Place of the Sun (Page 29-40)

Words to Know:

1. retrieving- to search for, find, and bring back
2. settlement- a newly colonized region.
3. trailing- to follow behind.
4. solstice- either of two times of the year when the sun is at its greatest angular distance from Earth's equator.
5. Summer Solstice- in the Northern Hemisphere, the summer solstice occurs about June 21 and is the longest day of the year.
6. Winter Solstice- in the Northern Hemisphere, the winter solstice occurs about December 21 and is the shortest day of the year.
7. scarcity- insufficiency of amount or supply; shortage.
8. surname- a name shared in common to identify the members of a family, as distinguished from each member's given name. Also called family name, last name.
9. corral- an enclosure for confining livestock.
10. retaliate- to do something in response to an action done to oneself or an associate, especially to attack or injure someone as a response to a hurtful action.
11. mete- to distribute or allot.
12. designated- to indicate or specify; point out.
13. procession- a group of persons, vehicles, or objects moving along in an orderly, formal manner.
14. pursued- to follow in an effort to overtake or capture; chase.
15. projectiles- a fired, thrown, or otherwise propelled object, such as a bullet, having no capacity for self-propulsion.
16. severed- to cut off (a part) from a whole.
17. abandoned- left behind, deserted; forsaken.
18. converged- to come together from different directions; meet.
19. shackles- a device, usually one of a pair connected to a chain that encircles the ankle or wrist of a prisoner or captive.
20. pouches- a small bag often closing with a drawstring and used especially for carrying loose items in one's pocket.
21. assortment- a collection of various kinds; a variety.

Questions:

1. Limik knows the horses will be a valuable food source for his people. How do Kilik and Malik convince Limik the horses are more valuable alive?
   - They tell them they have learned to ride these animals and that they could be useful for scouting larger areas.
2. Why did the group take on surnames (last names)? Which surname did each family take and why?
   - This would complete their disguises as Mexicans.
   - Tuhuy took the name, Solares. Kilik took the name, De La Tierra.
3. Why did Kilik think it was necessary to attack the caravan Malik spotted? Why did Tukuyun not want to attack the caravan at first?
   - They wanted to free the Indian captives.
   - Tukuyun thought it was too dangerous and didn't want to lose men.
4. Why do you think the Natives were surprised and delighted to see firearms and ammunition even though they did not know how to use them?
   - Knew the firearms were powerful tools.
   - Kept the firearms from their enemies.

Chapter 4- Musket Balls and Gunpowder (Page 41-54)

Words to Know:

1. extensive- large in extent, range, or amount.
2. absolute- not to be doubted or questioned; positive.
3. vigorously- Characterized by or done with force and energy.
4. *Si, senor, inmediatamente, senor* (Spanish)- Yes sir, immediately, sir
5. venison- the flesh of a deer used as food.
6. convinced- to cause (someone) by the use of argument or evidence to believe something or to take a course of action.
7. prejudiced- a judgment or opinion against something or someone formed unfairly or without knowledge of the facts.
8. ignorance- the condition of being uneducated, unaware, or uninformed.
9. *Tonto* (Spanish name given to captured Mexican)- fool or stupid
10. chatty- inclined to chat; friendly and talkative.
11. rambling- lengthy and digressive.
12. *vaquero* (Spanish)- cowboy
13. *rancho* (Spanish)- ranch
14. pitted- to set in direct opposition or competition.
15. captive- one, such as a prisoner of war, who is forcibly confined, subjugated, or enslaved.
16. translator- an interpreter.
17. frustration- the act of preventing the accomplishment or fulfillment of something.
18. musket rifle- a smoothbore, single-shot, shoulder gun used from the late 1500s through the early 1800s.
19. simultaneously- happening, existing, or done at the same time.
20. muzzle- the forward, discharging end of the barrel of a firearm.
21. glared- to stare fixedly and angrily.

Questions:

1. Why does Kilik demand the Mexican man give him his shoes?
    - He wants to complete his disguise.
2. Why did Kilik not want to kill the Mexican? What information could he have about the strangers that would be helpful to the Natives?
    - The prisoner would be able to tell them about the Mexican people and what they are doing in the region.

- He knows where the towns are located and how they move from one location to another.
3. What name is given to the stranger? Who suggests the name and why does he give it to the prisoner?
    - Solomol suggests calling him Tonto because the padres had called native people this when they didn't understand.
4. In what way will the prisoner help the Native people? Why is Malik chosen to work with the prisoner?
    - Answer questions about the strangers and show them how to use the firearms.
    - Malik was chosen to speak to the prisoner because he spoke Spanish
5. What was used as a target while the Natives learned how to use the firearms?
    - Tonto's hat.

Chapter 5- The Monterey Plan (Page 55-62)

Words to Know:

1. impending- to be about to occur.
2. domestic- a household servant.
3. *Ay caramba!* (Spanish)- Oh no!
4. loincloth- A strip of cloth worn around the loins.
5. *Oh, Dios Mio!* (Spanish)- Oh, my goodness or oh, my god.
6. intuition- the faculty of knowing or understanding something without reasoning or proof.
7. intuitive- Of, relating to, or arising from intuition.
8. ailments- A physical or mental disorder, especially a mild illness.
9. bustling- Excited and often noisy activity; a stir.
10. gag- Something forced into or put over the mouth to prevent speaking or crying out.
11. *Ese Indio escapado!* (Spanish)- That Indian escaped!

Questions:

1. Why does Malik want to go to Monterey?
   - Malik missed being a vaquero and heard there were jobs there.
2. Alapay also wants to go to Monterey, what reason does she give her father, Tuhuy, for wanting to go live there?
   - Alapay enjoyed her job working in the house.
   - Alapay tells her father she will be learning about the strange new people
3. What did the cousins do with Tonto when they arrived in Monterey?
   - Dressed Tonto as a native, put him on a horse and sent the horse running through town.
4. How were the guns captured both useful and useless to the people at the Place of the Sun?
   - Helped make hunting easier.
   - Ran out of gunpowder and could no longer be used.

Chapter 6- Mateo and Andrea (Page 63-74)

Words to Know:

1. lampposts- a post supporting a street lamp.
2. *Ingles* (Spanish)- English (language)
3. rounded- shaped into the form of a circle or sphere; made round.
4. embrace- to clasp or hold close with the arms, usually as an expression of affection.
5. *Rancho Buena Vista* (Spanish)- Good View Ranch
6. foreman- a man who serves as the leader of a work crew, as on a ranch or in a factory.
7. lasso- to catch, tie, or attach with or as if with a lasso.
8. riddled- to pierce with numerous holes; perforate.
9. plague- to cause suffering or hardship for.
10. fondness- having a strong liking, inclination, or affection.

Questions:

1. Why would Alapay and Malik, not know that Monterey is the capital of Alta California?
   - They have been living in a village far away.
   - They have never been there before.
2. What was Alapay's surprise when she went looking for work at Mr. Larkin's?
   - Her old friend Magdalena worked there.
3. Malik was not happy about his new job offer, why did he think he should take it anyway?
   - He would be valuable as a spy for his village.
4. What ceremony does Yol ask Tuhuy to perform? Why does Tuhuy have concerns about performing it?
   - Condor Vision ceremony.
   - He has not performed the ceremony in a long time and is worried it will not work.

Chapter 7- The Cowboy and the Maid (Page 75-84)

Words to Know:

1. stooping- to bend forward and down from the waist or the middle of the back.
2. *Mariposa* (Malik's wife-Spanish)- butterfly
3. fateful- controlled by or as if by fate; predetermined.
4. marshes- an area of low-lying land that is usually saturated with water and is dominated by herbaceous rather than woody plants.
5. tributaries- a stream that flows into a larger stream or other body of water.
6. quarters- a place of residence, especially the buildings or barracks used to house military personnel or dependents.
7. mending- clothes and other articles that must be repaired.
8. phrases- a sequence of words that have meaning, especially when forming part of a sentence.
9. customs house- the office at a port or frontier where customs duty is collected.
10. wagers- a matter bet on; a gamble.
11. grove- a small wood or stand of trees lacking dense undergrowth.
12. expeditions- an outing undertaken with a definite objective
13. concluded- to bring to an end; close.
14. bolted- to move or spring suddenly.
15. cluster- a group of the same or similar elements gathered or occurring closely together; a bunch.
16. jockeying- to maneuver for a certain position or advantage.
17. trampled- to beat down with the feet so as to crush, bruise, or destroy; tramp on.
18. gasps- to draw in the breath sharply, as from shock.
19. spectators- an observer of an event, especially a sports contest.
20. beaming- to smile expansively.

Questions:

1. What does Magdalena teach Alapay, and what does this allow her to do around town?
    - Teach her to read in Spanish.

2. What was the Native woman's name and why was Malik (Mateo) not supposed to talk to her?
   - Mariposa / Natives were not allowed to talk to Mexicans and Malikk was pretending to be a Mexican vaquero.
3. What happened to Magdalena's father? Why did she leave her home?
   - After the Indians escaped he became more bitter and unforgiving.
   - She did not like being around him.
4. Why does Mateo (Malik) start off lagging in the race?
   - To avoid being pushed and shoved; trampled.

Chapter 8- The Falcon Rides Again (Page 85-94)

Words to Know:

1. gobbling- to take greedily; grab.
2. citizenry- citizens considered as a group.
3. horsemanship- the skill of riding horses; equitation.
4. scanned- to look at carefully or thoroughly, especially in search of something; examine.
5. spurting- a sudden forcible gush or jet.
6. gazing- to look steadily, intently, and with fixed attention.
7. militias- an army composed of ordinary citizens rather than professional soldiers.
8. turmoil- a state of extreme confusion or agitation; commotion or tumult.
9. engulf- to swallow up or overwhelm by or as if by overflowing and enclosing.
10. aye- an affirmative vote, yes.
11. heathens- one who is regarded as irreligious, uncivilized, or unenlightened.
12. saddling- to put a saddle onto.
13. barbaric- marked by crudeness or lack of sophistication.

Questions:

1. What problems did Native people face as the strangers spread out further across the countryside?
   - Gobbling up ancestral hunting and food gathering land.
2. During the raid at Rancho Buena Vista, why did Mateo have to fire his weapon?
   - So the vaqueros would not think he was one of the natives.
3. Why were Mexican militias formed? Were these militias fair? Why or why not?
   - Militias were formed to retaliate against raids.
   - Raids often did not seek justice; slaughtered any Natives they found.
4. Why are the rancheros going to raid Tukuyun's village? What does Mateo (Malik) know he must do?
   - Punishment for the raid.
   - Malik must leave and warn the village.
5. How does Mateo (Malik) convince Mariposa to leave with him?
   - Tells her he loves and wants to marry her.

Chapter 9- New Rulers New Laws (Page 95-104)

Words to Know:

1. dismounted- to get down from a horse or other steed.
2. paste- a soft, smooth, thick mixture or material.
3. various- of diverse, different kinds.
4. uproot- to force to leave an accustomed or native location.
5. fortified- to strengthen and secure (a position) with fortifications.
6. refugees- one who flees, especially to another country, seeking refuge from war, political oppression, religious persecution, or a natural disaster.
7. vantage- a position, condition, or opportunity that is likely to provide superiority or an advantage.
8. flora- plants considered as a group, especially the plants of a particular country, region, or time.
9. fauna- animals, especially the animals of a particular region or period, considered as a group.
10. ligaments- a sheet or band of tough, fibrous tissue connecting bones or cartilages at a joint or supporting an organ.
11. sling- a weapon consisting of a looped strap in which a stone is whirled and then let fly.
12. arc- something shaped like a curve or arch.
13. anew- once more; again.
14. impact- to have an effect on.
15. nugget- a small, solid lump, especially of gold.
16. inhabitants- one that lives in a place, especially as a permanent resident.
17. legislature- an officially elected or otherwise selected body of people with the responsibility and power to make laws for a political unit, such as a state or nation.

Questions:

1. Why is Malik concerned about his father?
   - He knew he was shot in the raid.
2. What problems did other Yokuts, who had already tried to move east, face?
   - Disease and draught have taken a toll on food sources.
3. Who does Mariposa think can help the villagers?
   - Her tribe, the Miwok.

4. What had changed since Mariposa had been away from her tribe? How could this be a problem for the travelers?
   - John Sutter, s Swiss immigrant, built a fortified settlement.
   - Made travel more dangerous.
5. Why was Tuhuy so delighted to meet Loknee?
   - Both of their names are Rain; Loknee means rain coming through, Tuhuy means rain.
6. How did Kilik adapt to fighting after his injury left him unable to shoot a bow?
   - He started to use a sling.
7. What did living among the Miwok people allow Tuhuy and Alapay to do?
   - They reconnected with nature and spiritual practices.
8. Name the law that allowed white settlers to kidnap, sell or enslave Native American people.
   - Act for the Government and Protection of Indians.

Chapter 10- A War of Extermination (Page 105-114)

Words to Know:

1. mass murder- the deaths of many individuals.
2. fascinated- to capture and hold someone's interest and attention.
3. prompted- to give rise to; inspire.
4. ignorance- the condition of being uneducated, unaware, or uninformed.
5. civilized- showing evidence of moral and intellectual advancement; humane, ethical, and reasonable.
6. extermination- to get rid of by destroying completely.
7. extinct- no longer existing or living.
8. expenditure- the act or process of spending money.
9. frustrated- to cause feelings of discouragement, annoyance, or lack of fulfillment.
10. sloshed- to agitate in a liquid.
11. silt- a sedimentary material consisting of very fine particles intermediate in size between sand and clay.
12. strained- done with or marked by excessive effort; forced.

Questions:

1. Who was Henry Jamieson and why was he fascinated with indigenous people?
   - Newspaper reporter.
   - Fascinated with indigenous people that had lived for generations without ruining the land.
   - He didn't believe they are sub-humans like many others did.
2. What prejudiced views had Henry heard about Indians?
   - They will sneak up and rob you in your sleep.
   - They are untrustworthy.
3. Why does the newspaper editor tell Henry the newspaper will not print stories about how bad Indians were being treated?
   - Most readers wanted to hear about the booming economy because of gold.
4. How was Alapay able to understand what the white men who were hunting for gold were saying?
   - She had learned English from Magdalena while she stayed at Mr. Larkin's.
5. What happened to the white men?
   - There was a gun fight between two groups of white men.

Chapter 11- Death at Dawn (Page 115-124)

Words to Know:

1. murmur- a low, indistinct, continuous sound:
2. hostile- of, relating to, or characteristic of an enemy.
3. consulted- to seek advice or information of.
4. provisions- the act of making preparations for a possible or future event or situation.
5. hulls- the main body of various structures or other large vehicles, such as a tank, airship, or flying boat.
6. flee- to run away, as from trouble or danger.
7. ghastly- causing shock, revulsion, or horror; terrifying.
8. erupted- to develop suddenly.
9. cautiously- showing or practicing caution; careful.
10. saddlebags- a pair of pouches hanging across the back of a horse behind the saddle.

Questions:

1. Why did Malik and Alapay travel to neighboring tribes' villages?
   - They knew how to ride horses, making the trip faster.
   - Send word to neighboring tribes about the trouble the new white strangers have brought.
2. What is the big announcement Malik and Mariposa share with the village?
   - They will be having a child.
3. How does Malik know the attack on the village was by surprise?
   - The men died without weapons in their hands.
4. How does Alapay know this attack was done by the white strangers?
   - She called on her spirit helper to reveal what had happened
   - I mages began to appear to her of the events that took place
5. Why does Alapay and Malik attack Henry when they first meet?
   - They think he may be with the group that attacked the village.
6. What does Henry hope to learn from staying in Alapay and Malik's village?
   - He wants to record what the white men are doing in their native lands.

Chapter 12- Follow Orders (Page 125-136)

Words to Know:

1. gesturing- a motion of the limbs or body made to express or help express thought or to emphasize speech.
2. *vamanos* (Spanish)- Let's go
3. peering- to look intently, searchingly, or with difficulty.
4. belched- to expel gas noisily.
5. troughs- a long, narrow, generally shallow receptacle for holding water or feed for animals.
6. plunged- to dive, jump, or throw oneself.
7. Eureka- used to express triumph upon finding or discovering something.
8. echoed- repetition of a sound by reflection of sound waves from a surface.
9. vigilance- alert watchfulness.
10. flint- a very hard, fine-grained quartz that sparks when struck with steel.
11. wad- a small mass of soft material, often folded or rolled, used for padding, stuffing, or packing.
12. kindling- easily ignited material, such as dry sticks of wood, used to start a fire.
13. mischievous- playful in a naughty or teasing way.
14. banter- good-humored, playful, or teasing conversation.
15. dreaded- causing terror or fear.
16. thread- to make (one's way) cautiously through something.
17. brandished- to wave or flourish (something, often a weapon) in a menacing, defiant, or excited way.
18. stockade- a jail on a military base or an area to keep animals.

Questions:

1. What did Malik mean when he said, "I know I'm going to be sick", to Alapay?
   - He is teasing her because she likes Henry
2. What did Malik say to Henry that surprised Alapay?
   - Called him friend.
3. Why was the salmon Malik speared so particularly good?
   - They had been eating only dried food.
   - Fresh meal.
4. Where were the cousins when they noticed the faded images? Why was this important to Alapay?
   - The cousins were in a cave.

- The cave paintings reminded Alapay of Tuhuy teaching her Chumash symbols and their purpose.
5. How did the cousins know the men with soldier uniforms on were not Mexican?
   - They were white men.
   - Rode with a red and white triangular flag.
   - They wore blue uniforms.
6. Why are the cousins worried no one back in the village will believe what they have seen?
   - Hard for them to believe what they have seen with their own eyes.
   - Doesn't seem possible.

Chapter 13- Pay Good Money (Page 137-148)

Words to Know:

1. massacre- the act or an instance of killing a large number of humans indiscriminately and cruelly.
2. wadded- to compress into a wad.
3. fascinating- possessing the power to charm or allure; captivating.
4. dispersed- to separate and move in different directions; scatter.
5. awkward- clumsily or unskillfully performed.
6. clumsy- lacking physical coordination, skill, or grace; awkward.
7. column- something resembling an architectural column in form.
8. welt- a lash or blow producing such a mark.
9. *Hablo solo Espanol* (Spanish)- I only speak Spanish.
10. squaw- offensive slang, a Native American woman, especially a wife.
11. bluffing- to engage in a false display of confidence or aggression in order to deceive or intimidate someone.
12. holster- a case of leather or similar material into which a pistol fits snugly and attaches to a belt, strap, or saddle so that it may be carried or transported.
13. revolver- a handgun having a revolving cylinder with several cartridge chambers that may be fired in succession.
14. scurried- to go with light running steps; scamper.

Questions:

1. Why wouldn't the editor publish Henry's story? What did this cause Henry to do?
   - Said the readers would not be interested in it.
   - Henry quit his job to write the book he always wanted to write.
2. What does Tuhuy say about trusting a white man? What does Alapay say to change his mind?
   - You can't trust a white man.
   - Alapay tells her father she has met another nice white man like Mr. Larkin who was respectful to Indians.
3. How did Alapay know, without seeing, the camp was not Henry's?
   - She heard more than one voice.
   - Henry would be alone.
4. What does Henry tell the men to try and set Alapay free?
   - That she belongs to him because he paid for her.

Chapter 14- Eyes of the Condor (Page 149-158)

Words to Know:

1. dumbfounded- to fill with astonishment and perplexity; confound.
2. *perdoname* (Spanish)- excuse me.
3. utmost- of the highest or greatest degree, amount, or intensity; most extreme.
4. admiration- a feeling of strong approval or delight with regard to someone or something.
5. speculate- to engage in a course of reasoning often based on inconclusive evidence; conjecture or theorize.
6. absorb- to learn; acquire.
7. jotting- a brief note or memorandum.
8. phases- a distinct stage of development.
9. verbalized- to express in words.
10. parallel- moving in the same direction at a fixed interval.
11. maneuvered- a movement or combination of movements involving skill and dexterity.
12. miraculously- of the nature of a miracle.

Questions:

1. What greeting gestures by Henry were unfamiliar to the people in the village?
   - Handshake.
   - Kissing a woman's hand.
2. How is Henry a new source of information for the people in the village?
   - He is a white man.
   - He has lived in their cities and know of plan for further expansion.
3. Why doesn't Tuhuy use the Eye of the Condor ceremony to see if they can return to the Place of River Turtles?
   - He wasn't able to perform the ceremony last three times he tried.
4. How does Alapay begin to prepare for the Eye of the Condor ceremony?
   - The night before, stay quiet and focus her energy.
   - Day of, multiple cycles of prayer and song.
5. What did Alapay take with her for the ceremony?
   - Tule reed mat.
   - Basket water bottle.
6. How did Alapay recognize the Place of River Turtles during the ceremony?
   - Her father had described where the Place or River Turtles was located.

Chapter 15- The Long Journey Home (Page 159- 168)

Words to Know:

1. anxiously- uneasy and apprehensive about an uncertain event or matter; worried.
2. *timolokich* (Chumash)- a story.
3. *que bueno* (Spanish)- That's good or that's great.
4. slopes- a stretch of ground forming a natural or artificial incline.
5. ferries- a place where passengers or goods are transported across a body of water, such as a river or bay, by a ferryboat.
6. cowering- to cringe in fear.
7. volley- a simultaneous discharge of a number of bullets or other projectiles.
8. steed- a horse, especially a spirited one.
9. fluttering- to wave or flap rapidly in an irregular manner.

Questions:

1. Why do Solomol and Yol want to return to their home village?
   - They are getting older and it would mean a lot to be able to see their old home.
2. Why does Henry's plan cause anger at first? Who convinces the elders to think about it?
   - His plan suggests they pretend to be his slaves.
   - Malik tells Kilik it will only be a story, *timolokich*, when they encounter Mexicans or Americans.
3. How will Henry's plan help the villagers as they travel?
   - Avoid conflicts with other travelers.
   - They will be able to take faster routes.
4. What made it possible, as Kilik said, for the travelers to have survived the outlaws attack?
   - Planning, preparation and practice.

Chapter 16- The Place of River Turtles (Page 169-180)

Words to Know:

1. odyssey- an extended adventurous voyage or trip.
2. territory- an area of land; a region.
3. ruins- the state of being physically destroyed, collapsed, or decayed.
4. adobe- a building material consisting of clay mixed with straw or dung, fashioned into sun-dried bricks or used as mortar or plaster.
5. dilapidated- having fallen into a state of disrepair or deterioration, as through neglect; broken-down and shabby.
6. ravaged- to bring heavy destruction on; devastate.
7. decrepit- weakened, worn out, impaired, or broken down by old age, illness, or hard use.
8. raspy- rough; grating.
9. rubble- a loose mass of angular fragments of rock or masonry crumbled by natural or human forces.
10. *haku* (Chumash)- hello
11. *lo siento, no entiendo* (Spanish)- I'm sorry, I do not understand.
12. knoll- a small rounded hill or mound; a hillock.
13. prying- insistently or impertinently curious or inquisitive.

Questions:

1. Why was Kai-ina able to guide them as they continued south?
    - Recognized landmarks from her time living with the Yokuts.
2. How do Solomol and Kilik respond when the padre offered to rent a room?
    - They said No, they wouldn't stay there if you paid them.
3. At the ruins of Mission Santa Ines, why does Solomol want to go inside? Once inside, why does he make an offering?
    - It makes his heart feel good to see it in ruins.
    - Offers a blessing song for the hundreds of Chumash who are buried there.
4. Why was the offering at the mission so important to the group?
    - Began a small bit of healing.
5. Why didn't the native people they encountered speak their native languages?
    - After living at the missions so long no one knew the language anymore.
6. What happened to Henry and why didn't Alapay leave with him?
    - Spent several months writing his book about the Native people.
    - Asked Alapay to go with him; She said no, her place was with her people.

Language Arts/ History/ Social Science
Extension Projects and Activities

The following activities are suggestions for further learning and can deepen the connection between the narrative and real historical events in California's History. Attached to each suggested activity are some basic California learning standards for referencing.

- **Comic Strip Story Map**
  The elements of a story assist students in their understanding of what is taking place in the novel. When students comprehend the story elements of characters, setting, problems, events, and solutions, they become more involved in the story and take a greater interest. In this lesson, students use a 12-panel comic strip to create a story map. The story strips that result provide a great way to evaluate student's understanding of important events and elements in a novel.

  (Materials needed: construction paper, colored pencils/ markers/crayons, scissors, glue)

  -Common Core ELA Standards: CCSS.ELA-LITERACY.RL.4.1 CCSS.ELA-LITERACY.W.4.4

- **Triangle Diorama: The Four Basic Elements of a Story**
  A simple yet effective way to check for basic elemental understanding of a story. As a whole group, students will discuss the elements of the story prior to beginning the activity. Project should feature their understanding of story elements as well as present their creative interpretation. *Triangle diorama project instructions can be found online.*

    - Students represent four story elements, one per triangle diorama, creating a full square art piece representing student learning. (Plot, Characters, Setting, Theme)
    - Student art should be open to the student's interpretation of the story element being represented.
    - Attach student writing to the bottom of each triangle. Student writing should demonstrate understanding of the story elements in connection with the story and include an explanation of their art.

- (Materials needed: construction paper, colored pencils/ markers/crayons, scissors, glue)

-Common Core ELA Standards: CCSS.ELA-LITERACY.RL.4.2, CCSS.ELA-LITERACY.RL.4.3

- **Mapping the characters journey throughout California.**
  As the story is either read whole class or individually, come back as a group and discuss the routes taken by the lead characters. Using a large classroom map or individual electronic devices, plot the journey and discuss what hardships might be found, in not only the terrain, but also the resources. (Materials needed: Large classroom map or individual electronic devices)
    - On a large classroom map, have students plot California locations as characters travel throughout the state. *Technology Variation: Track locations on an internet-based mapping program.
    - Plot major Mexican and American Cities and settlements mentioned in the story.
    - Discuss routes taken by the story characters to elude detection and the major roadways used by the Mexicans and Americans. What made these routes possible? Which are still in use to this day?
    - Discuss the flora and fauna of each region. Students create flip books highlighting key features of each region. *Technology Variation: Students create interactive notes using a web-based slideshow program. Each slide can contain anything valuable to the student pertaining to a particular region including notes, pictures, video and links.
    - Discuss the Native regions and homelands as the characters move in and out of neighboring tribal lands. Students create flip books highlighting key features of home construction and clothing. *Technology Variation: Students create interactive notes using a web-based slideshow program. Each slide can contain anything valuable to the student pertaining to a particular region including notes, pictures, video and links.

-History-Social Science Content Standards: 4.1.5; 4.2.1; 4.3.1; 4.3.2

- **Journal Writing**
  - Alapay found great power in the ability to read, and Henry wanted his words to inform; our future needs to know this value.
    - Have students take on the role of Alapay. How is Alapay constantly learning throughout the story? What value do they see in keeping traditions going from one generation to the next?
    - Have the students take on the role of Henry. What do they want to tell the world about these native people they have been learning about? What value do they see in preserving this culture that was once threatened by extinction?

-Common Core ELA Standards: CCSS.ELA-LITERACY.W.4.1, CCSS.ELA-LITERACY.W.4.2, CCSS.ELA-LITERACY.W.4.3

www.ingramcontent.com/pod-product-compliance
Lightning Source LLC
Chambersburg PA
CBHW060520300426
44112CB00017B/2736